A
SCOTT
FORESMAN
Adventure

Reading STREET

Program Authors

Peter Afflerbach

Camille Blachowicz

Candy Dawson Boyd

Wendy Cheyney

Connie Juel

Edward Kame'enui

Donald Leu

Jeanne Paratore

P. David Pearson

Sam Sebesta

Deborah Simmons

Sharon Vaughn

Susan Watts-Taffe

Karen Kring Wixson

PEARSON

Scott
Foresman

Editorial Offices: Glenview, Illinois • Parsippany, New Jersey • New York, New York
Sales Offices: Needham, Massachusetts • Duluth, Georgia • Glenview, Illinois
Coppell, Texas • Sacramento, California • Mesa, Arizona

About the Cover Artist

When Scott Gustafson was in grade school, he spent most of his spare time drawing pictures. Now he gets to make pictures for a living. Before he starts a painting, he photographs his family, pets, or friends posing as characters that will appear in the illustration. He then uses the photos to inspire the finished picture. In this cover you can see his pet cockatiel, Piper.

ISBN: 0-328-10833-2

4 5 6 7 8 9 10 V063 14 13 12 11 10 09 08 07 06

Dear Reader,

A new school year is beginning. Are you ready? You are about to take a trip along a famous street—*Scott Foresman Reading Street*. During this trip you will travel in space with some astronauts. You will explore the desert. You will go camping with Henry and his big dog Mudge. You will even build a robot with good friends Pearl and Wagner.

As you read these stories and articles, you will learn new things that will help you in science and social studies.

While you are enjoying these exciting pieces of literature, you will find that something else is going on—you are becoming a better reader.

Have a great trip, and don't forget to write!

Sincerely,
The Authors

Exploration

What can we learn from exploring new places and things?

Read It ONLINE sfsuccessnet.com

Contents

Working Together

How can we work together?

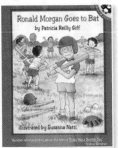

UNIT 3

Contents

Creative Ideas

Read It
ONLINE
sfsuccessnet.com

What does it mean to be creative?

8

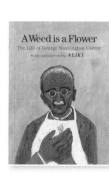

Exploration

What can we learn from exploring new places and things?

Read It
ONLINE
sfsuccessnet.com

Let's Talk About
EXPLORATION

Words to Read

country
beautiful
front
someone
somewhere
friend

Read the Words

Iris and her family have moved to the country. It is a beautiful place. Iris looked at the long road in front of her house. She hopes that someone out there somewhere is waiting to be her friend.

Genre: Realistic Fiction

Realistic fiction is a made-up story that could happen in real life. Now read about Iris, a girl who moves to the country and finds a new friend.

Iris and Walter

by Elissa Haden Guest

illustrated by Christine Davenier

What new things does Iris learn
when she moves to the country?

A Walk and a Talk

Iris and Grandpa went for a walk.

"Can I tell you something?" Iris asked.

"You can tell me anything," said Grandpa.

"I hate the country," said Iris.

"Why?" asked Grandpa.

"Because there are no children here," said Iris. "The country is as lonely as Mars."

"Iris, my girl, there must be some
children somewhere," said Grandpa.
"Do you think so?" asked Iris.
"I know so. We shall have
to find them, Iris. We shall
be explorers!"

Iris and Grandpa walked down the road. The birds were singing. The roses were blooming. And around the bend, someone was waiting.

Iris and Grandpa walked around the
bend. They saw a great big green tree.
"What a tree!" said Grandpa.
"So green!" said Iris.
"So beautiful," said Grandpa.
"I want to climb it," said Iris.

Down came a ladder.

"Amazing! I wonder what's up there?" said Grandpa.

"I'll go see," said Iris. Iris began to climb.

"How is it up there?" called Grandpa.

"It's very green!" yelled Iris.

Iris climbed higher and higher until she was almost at the top of the great big green tree.

"Grandpa?!" called Iris.
"There's a house up here."
"Amazing!" said Grandpa.

Iris knocked on the door.

"Come in," said a voice.

Iris opened the door.

"Hi, I'm Walter," said Walter.

"I'm Iris," said Iris.

Iris and Walter shook hands.

"Hey, Grandpa, there's a kid up here named Walter!" yelled Iris.

"How wonderful," said Grandpa.

And it was.

A New Life

Iris and Walter played every day. They
climbed trees. They rolled down hills.
They played hide-and-seek.

When it rained,
Walter showed Iris his
hat collection. And Iris
showed Walter how to
roller-skate—indoors.

Some days they rode
Walter's sweet pony, Sal.
Other days they sat on a fence
and watched a horse named
Rain running wild.

"Tell me about the big city," said Walter.

"Well," said Iris, "in the big city, there are lots and lots and lots of people."

"Ah," said Walter. "But in the country there are lots and lots and lots of stars."

Iris and Walter played every day. But still Iris dreamed of the big city. She dreamed of her noisy street and her wide front stoop.

She dreamed of tango music and of
roller-skating down long hallways.
But Iris was not sad.

For in the country, there were
red-tailed hawks and starry skies.

There were pale roses. And there was
cool grass beneath her feet. There was a
wild horse named Rain and a sweet pony
named Sal.

And across the meadow,
over the stream, high in a tree,
was a little house. And inside
there was a new friend. . . Walter.

34

Think and Share

Talk About It Stories can go on and on. What do you think Iris and Walter do next?

1. Use the pictures below to retell the story.

2. Where does *Iris and Walter* take place? How might the story be different if Iris and Walter had met in the city?

3. What did you predict Iris would find in the tree? Were you right? What other predictions did you make?

Look Back and Write Look back at page 19. What problem did Iris have? How did that change? Use details from the story to help you.

Meet the Author and Illustrator
Elissa Haden Guest

STARRING
ELISSA HADEN GUEST

Elissa Haden Guest likes big cities. She says, "New York was a very exciting place to grow up. You can walk for miles there without getting tired or bored because there's so much to see. Many of the streets are crowded with people and there's this terrific energy in the air."

Christine Davenier

Christine Davenier lives in France, where she grew up. She taught kindergarten for four years before attending art school. She has illustrated many children's books.

Read more books about Iris and Walter.

Iris and Walter
The Sleepover

WRITTEN BY Elissa Haden Guest
ILLUSTRATED BY Christine Davenier

Iris and Walter
True Friends

WRITTEN BY Elissa Haden Guest
ILLUSTRATED BY Christine Davenier

Morning Song

by Bobbi Katz

Today is a day to catch tadpoles.
Today is a day to explore.
Today is a day to get started.
Come on! Let's not sleep anymore.

Outside the sunbeams are dancing.
The leaves sing a rustling song.
Today is a day for adventures,
and I hope that you'll come along!

My Travel Tree

by Bobbi Katz

There are oh-so-many
kinds of trees—
apple, pear, pine—
but there is just one special tree
I feel is somehow mine.
Its branches form
such cozy nooks
for dreaming dreams
and reading books.
I sail to almost anywhere,
perched among the leaves up there.
If naming things were up to me,
I'd call this one my travel tree.

Sentences

A **sentence** is a group of words that tells a complete idea. The words are in an order that makes sense. A sentence begins with a capital letter. Many sentences end with a **period (.)**.

Iris and Walter went swimming.

This is a sentence. It tells a complete idea.

Sal the pony.

This is not a sentence. It does not tell a complete idea. It needs to tell what Sal the pony does or is.

Write **Using Sentences**

1. This is not a sentence.

Iris and Walter.

Make it a sentence. Tell something that Iris and Walter do. Don't forget to use a period.

· ·

2. Choose a sentence from the story that tells about the pony or the horse. Tell more about the animal you choose. Be sure your sentence tells a complete idea.

· ·

3. Write some sentences about a special time you had with your family or friends. Remember to begin and end each sentence correctly.

Let's Talk About

EXPLORATION

Words to Read

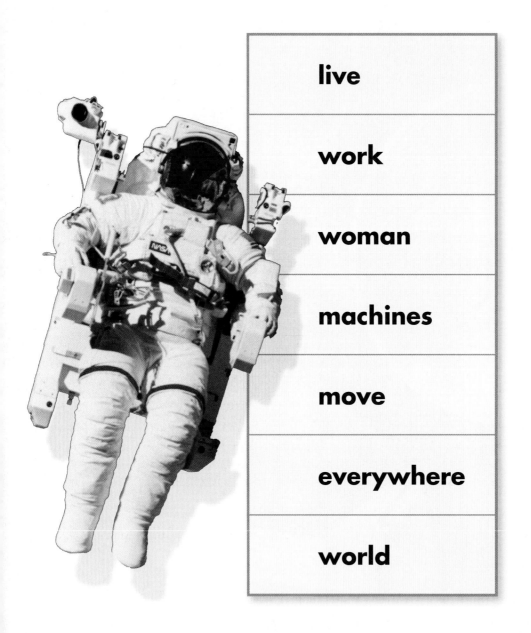

live
work
woman
machines
move
everywhere
world

Read the Words

Astronauts live and work in space.
A woman can be an astronaut.

Machines in space
can move
large things.

Stars are everywhere.
Can you see our world?

Genre: Expository Nonfiction
Expository nonfiction tells facts about a topic. Next you will read facts about the crew of a real space shuttle.

Exploring Space

with an Astronaut

by Patricia J. Murphy

What will you find out about space from an astronaut?

Lift-off!

3 . . . 2 . . . 1 . . . Lift-off!
A space shuttle climbs high into the sky. Inside the shuttle, astronauts are on their way to learn more about space.

What is an astronaut?

An astronaut is a person who goes into space. Astronauts fly on a space shuttle.

The space shuttle takes off like a rocket. It lands like an airplane.

United States

Meet Eileen Collins.

Eileen Collins is an astronaut. She was the first woman to be a space shuttle pilot. She was also the first woman to be the leader of a space shuttle trip.

She and four other astronauts worked as a team. Some astronauts flew the space shuttle. Others did experiments.

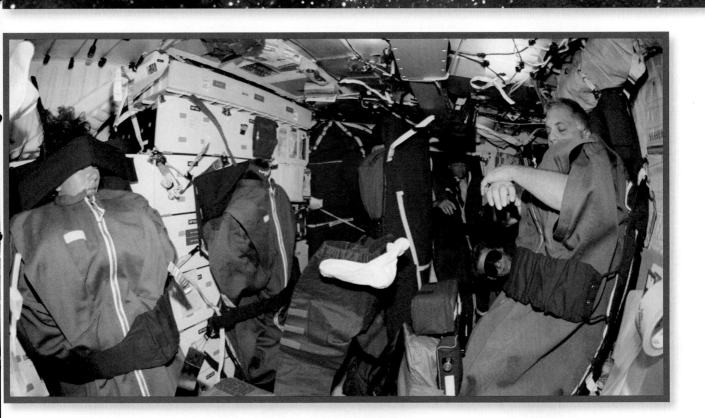

How do astronauts live in space?

In the space shuttle, astronauts float everywhere. Sleeping bags are tied to walls. Toilets have a type of seat belt.

Astronauts exercise to stay strong. They take sponge baths to keep clean.

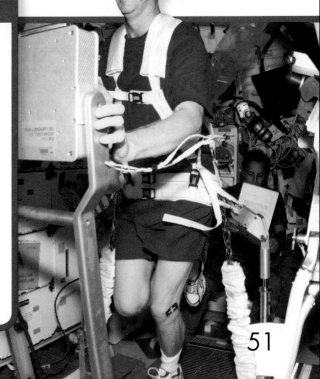

Why do astronauts go into space?

Astronauts test ways to live and work in a world that is very different from Earth. In space, there is no up and down, no air, and the sun always shines.

Astronauts do experiments. They look for problems and fix them. This will make space travel safer.

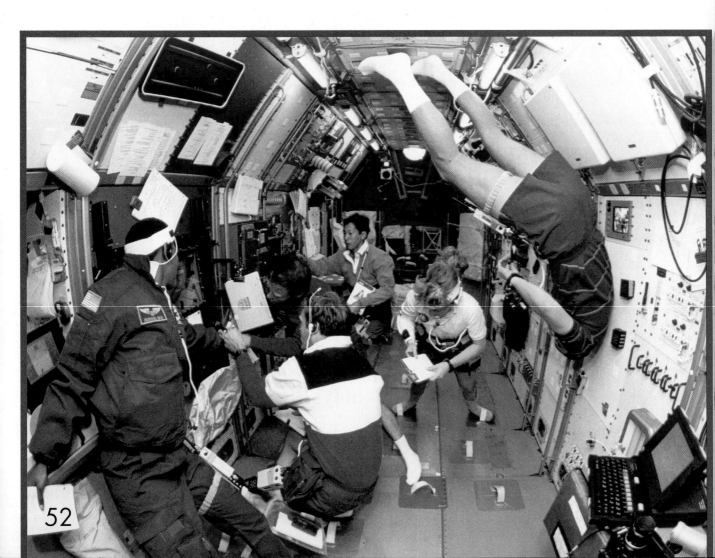

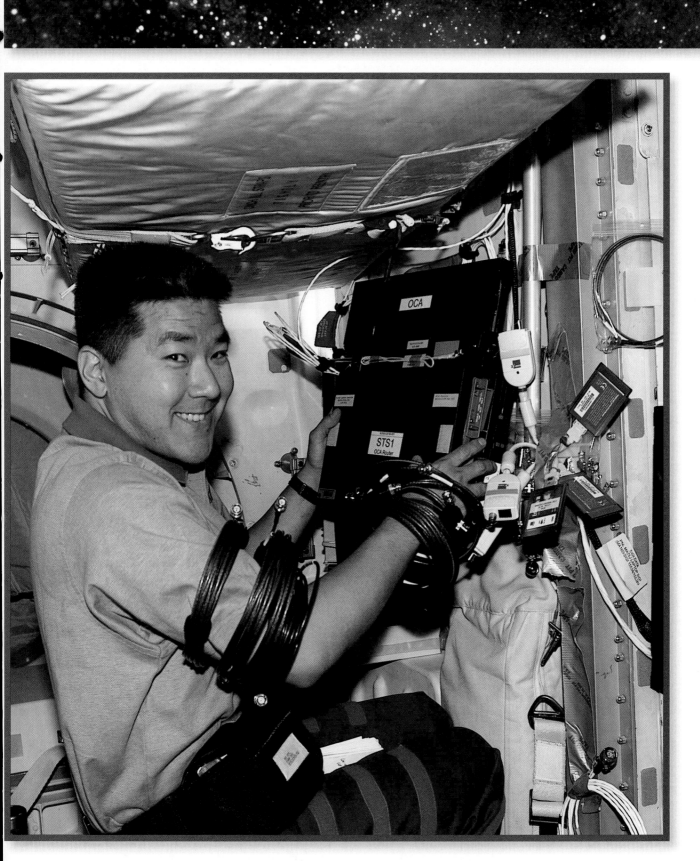

robot arm

space suit

What tools do astronauts use?

A space shuttle is a giant toolbox! It holds tools, such as computers, that help fly the space shuttle.

Astronauts use robot arms to move things and people outside the shuttle. On space walks, space suits keep astronauts safe.

X-ray telescope named *Chandra*

X-ray telescope

space shuttle

The crew's special job

Eileen Collins and her crew had a special job to do. They took an X-ray telescope into space with them.

First, they tested the telescope. Next, they flipped some switches and let the telescope go into space. Then, the telescope used its rockets to fly higher into space.

Did the astronauts do other jobs, too?

Yes. They did experiments with plants and exercise machines. They were studying life without gravity.

When there was some time to rest, the astronauts could look out their window. They saw Earth from many, many miles away!

Rocky Mountains in Colorado

plant experiment

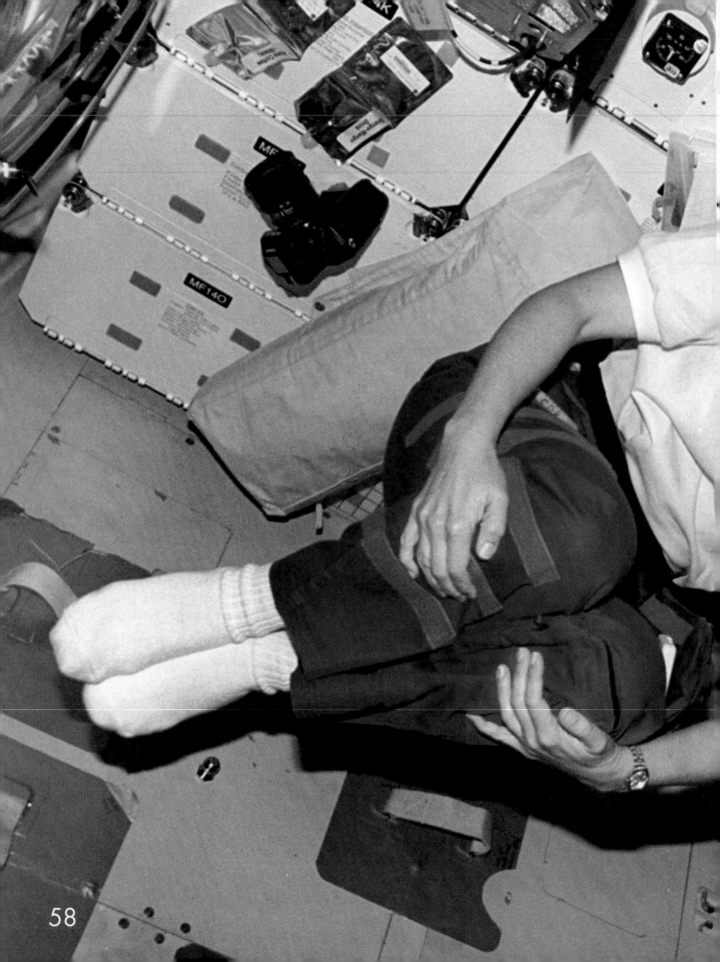

Would you like to fly into space?

Do you like math and science? Do you like to visit new places? Do you like fast roller coasters? Astronauts do, too! Maybe someday you will become an astronaut, just like Eileen Collins.

Think and Share

Talk About It You are an astronaut. Send a one-minute message to Earth. Tell about your trip.

1. Use the pictures below to summarize what you read about astronauts.

2. What do you think is the most important thing the author wanted you to know?

3. Most sections of this selection begin with a question. The next part answers the question. How did that format help you as you read?

Look Back and Write If you really want to be an astronaut, what things should you like? Look back on page 59 to help you answer.

Meet the Author
Patricia J. Murphy

Patricia Murphy likes everything about writing a book. When she starts a new book, she says, it's "fun and scary." When she's in the middle, her days are filled with "unexpected adventure and surprises—and a lot of mess and hard work." In the end, when the book is written, she feels excited and a little sad that it's all over. Then it's on to the next book!

Ms. Murphy is a writer and a photographer. She lives in Illinois.

Read more books by Patricia Murphy.

A Trip to Space Camp

by Ann Weil

What does it feel like to go into space? Would you like to find out? Then maybe Space Camp is for you!

There are all sorts of space camps that you could try. Some are for adults. Some are for teens. There is even a Space Camp for children as young as 7 years old. It is called Parent-Child Space Camp. Parent-Child Space Camp takes place over a long weekend. Families can go to Space Camp together.

Space Camp uses some of the same machines used to train real astronauts. There's a special chair that makes you feel like you are walking on the moon. Another chair is like the kind that astronauts use when they go outside their rocket ship to fix something. A third kind of chair makes you feel like you're floating in space. Still another machine spins you in circles and flips you head over heels. Then there's the Space Shot. The Space Shot shoots you straight into the air at about 45 to 50 miles per hour. You fall back down just as fast. Then you bump up and down a few times before it's over.

Y6 Gravity Chair

Working in Space

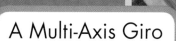

A Multi-Axis Giro

Everyone at space camp works together on special missions. On these missions you'll do work like real astronauts do in space. You might get to fly a rocket ship. It's only pretend, of course. You won't really fly into space. But it looks and feels like the real thing. And that's really fun!

Moon Gravity Chair

Subjects

. . . .

The **subject** of a sentence tells who or what does something.

. . . .

An astronaut goes into space.

An astronaut is the subject of the sentence.

Eileen Collins piloted the shuttle.

Eileen Collins is the subject of the sentence.

Write Using Subjects

1. Write a sentence from the selection. Underline the subject.

· ·

2. Choose a picture from the selection. Write a sentence about the picture. Underline the subject.

· ·

3. Astronauts do many everyday things aboard the space shuttle. Write some sentences about what you do every day. Underline the subject of each sentence you write.

Let's Talk About
Exploration

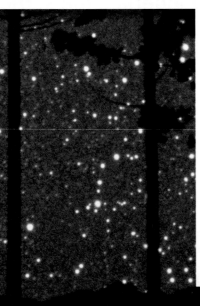

Words to Read

| love |
| mother |
| father |
| straight |
| bear |
| couldn't |
| build |

Read the Words

We all love camping. My mother and father take us camping every year. We go straight to the woods when we get there. Something new always happens on these trips. Last year, we saw a bear! I couldn't believe it. This year, my dad promised to teach us how to build a campfire. I can't wait!

Genre: Realistic Fiction Realistic fiction means that a story could happen. Next read about Henry and his dog, Mudge, and, their camping trip.

Henry and Mudge and the Starry Night

Henry and Mudge

and the Starry Night

by Cynthia Rylant

illustrated by Suçie Stevenson

What will Henry and Mudge find on a starry night?

Contents

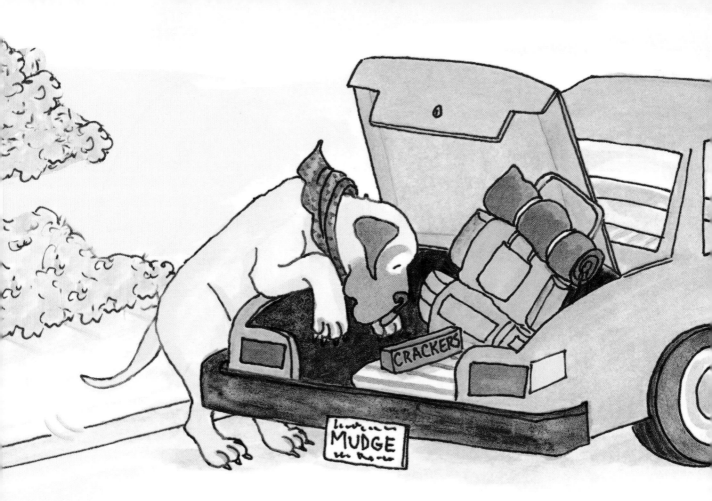

Big Bear Lake

In August Henry and Henry's big
dog Mudge always went camping.
They went with Henry's parents.

Henry's mother had been a Camp Fire Girl, so she knew all about camping.

She knew how to set up a tent.

She knew how to build a campfire. She
knew how to cook camp food.

Henry's dad didn't
know anything about
camping. He just
came with a guitar
and a smile.

Henry and Mudge loved camping. This year they were going to Big Bear Lake, and Henry couldn't wait.

"We'll see deer, Mudge," Henry said.
Mudge wagged.

"We'll see raccoons," said Henry.
Mudge shook Henry's hand.

"We might even see a *bear*," Henry said. Henry was not so sure he wanted to see a bear. He shivered and put an arm around Mudge.

Mudge gave a big, slow, *loud* yawn. He drooled on Henry's foot.

Henry giggled. "No bear will get *us*, Mudge," Henry said. "We're too *slippery!*"

A Good Smelly Hike

Henry and Mudge and Henry's parents drove
to Big Bear Lake. They parked the car and got
ready to hike.

Everyone had a backpack, even Mudge.
(His had lots of crackers.) Henry's mother said,
"Let's go!" And off they went.

They walked and walked and climbed and
climbed. It was beautiful.

Henry saw a fish jump straight out of a stream.
He saw a doe and her fawn. He saw waterfalls
and a rainbow.

81

Mudge didn't see much of anything. He was smelling. Mudge loved to hike and smell. He smelled a raccoon from yesterday. He smelled a deer from last night.

He smelled an oatmeal cookie from Henry's back pocket. "Mudge!" Henry laughed, giving Mudge the cookie.

Finally Henry's mother picked a good place to camp.

Henry's parents set up the tent. Henry
unpacked the food and pans and lanterns. Mudge
unpacked a ham sandwich. Finally the camp was
almost ready. It needed just one more thing:
"Who knows the words to 'Love Me Tender'?"
said Henry's father with a smile, pulling out his
guitar. Henry looked at Mudge and groaned.

Green Dreams

It was a beautiful night.

Henry and Henry's parents lay on their backs by the fire and looked at the sky. Henry didn't know there were so many stars in the sky.

"There's the Big Dipper," said Henry's mother.

"There's the Little Dipper," said Henry.

"There's E. T.," said Henry's dad.

Mudge wasn't looking at stars. He was chewing on a log. He couldn't get logs this good at home. Mudge loved camping.

Henry's father sang one more sappy love song, then everyone went inside the tent to sleep. Henry's father and mother snuggled. Henry and Mudge snuggled.

It was as quiet as quiet could be. Everyone slept safe and sound, and there were no bears, no scares. Just the clean smell of trees . . . and wonderful green dreams.

Think and Share

Talk About It Pretend you are Mudge. What were the best sights and smells on the camping trip?

1. Look at the pictures below. They are in the wrong order. Reorder them to retell the story.

2. Who are the characters in this story? Describe the setting.

3. Did anything in this story confuse you? What did you do about it?

Look Back and Write Look at page 76. Who knew all about camping? What did that person do to help with the camping trip? Use details from the story.

88

Meet the Author and the Illustrator
Cynthia Rylant

Cynthia Rylant never read many books when she was young. There was no library in her town.

Read more books by Cynthia Rylant.

After college, Ms. Rylant worked in a library. "Within a few weeks, I fell in love with children's books," she says. She has written over 60 books!

Suçie Stevenson

Suçie Stevenson has drawn pictures for most of the Henry and Mudge books. Her brother's Great Dane, Jake, was her inspiration for Mudge.

Star Pictures in the Sky

by Lorraine McCombs

Have you ever connected the dots to make a picture? Think about the stars in the sky. A long time ago, people saw the stars as dots in the night sky. They imagined lines going from star to star. They called these star pictures *constellations.*

On a very dark night away from the city, we can see hundreds of stars in the sky. We can even see the same constellations that people saw long ago. Here are a few of them.

This star picture, or constellation, is called Orion. It is named after a famous hunter in Greek stories. We see Orion best in the winter sky. This constellation has three stars in a row. They are thought of as Orion's belt.

The Big Dipper is a star picture in the constellation called Big Bear. We can see the Big Dipper any time of the year, but it is best seen between January and October. Two stars in the Big Dipper point toward the very bright North Star.

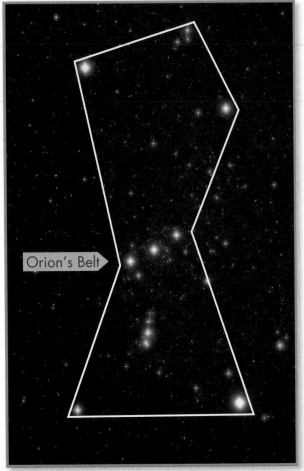

Orion's Belt

Orion

Big Dipper

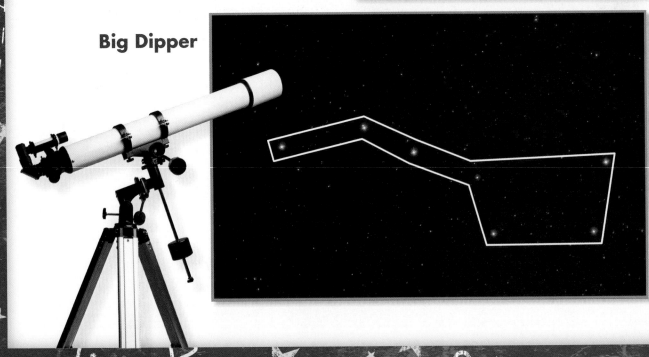

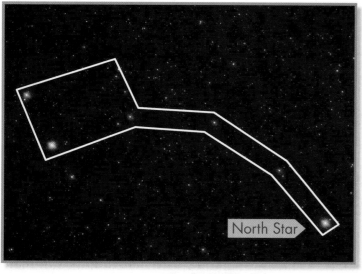

Little Dipper

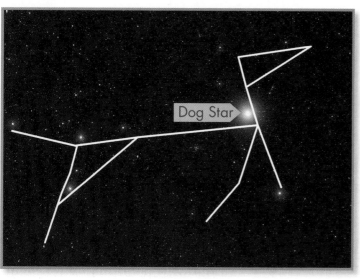

Big Dog

Another star picture is the Little Dipper. You can see the Little Dipper all year. Notice the handle. The brightest star in the handle is the North Star. It never moves. For hundreds of years, people have used the North Star to find their way.

Canis was a dog in Greek stories. *Canis* means "dog," and this constellation is known as the Big Dog. The very bright star is called the Dog Star. It is the brightest star in our whole nighttime sky. You can usually find this constellation in the summer sky between July and September.

The next time you look up at a dark, starry sky, think about these constellations. Connect the dots as people did long ago. What star pictures do you see?

Predicates

The **predicate** tells what the subject of a sentence does or is.

Henry and Mudge **walked down the trail.**

The words **walked down the trail** tell what Henry and Mudge did.

Henry's mom **is a hiker.**

The words **is a hiker** tell what Henry's mom is.

Write **Using Predicates**

1. Write a sentence from the story. Underline the predicate.

· ·

2. What would you do on a camping trip? Write a sentence about it. Underline the predicate in your sentence.

· ·

3. Write about a trip you have taken or would like to take. Tell what you did or will do. Tell what you saw or will see. Underline the predicate in each sentence.

Let's Talk About
EXPLORATION

Words to Read

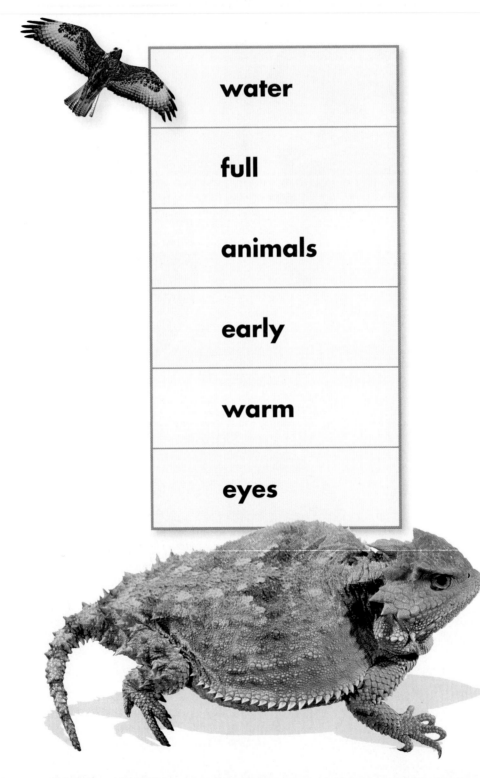

water
full
animals
early
warm
eyes

Read the Words

Some places on Earth have very little water. It is hot and dry, but these places are full of life. Plants and animals can live there. You can visit these places too. Go out early before the sun is too warm. Be sure to protect your eyes when you go out!

A Walk in the Desert

Genre: Expository Nonfiction

Expository nonfiction gives information about a topic. In the next selection, you will read about a walk in the desert.

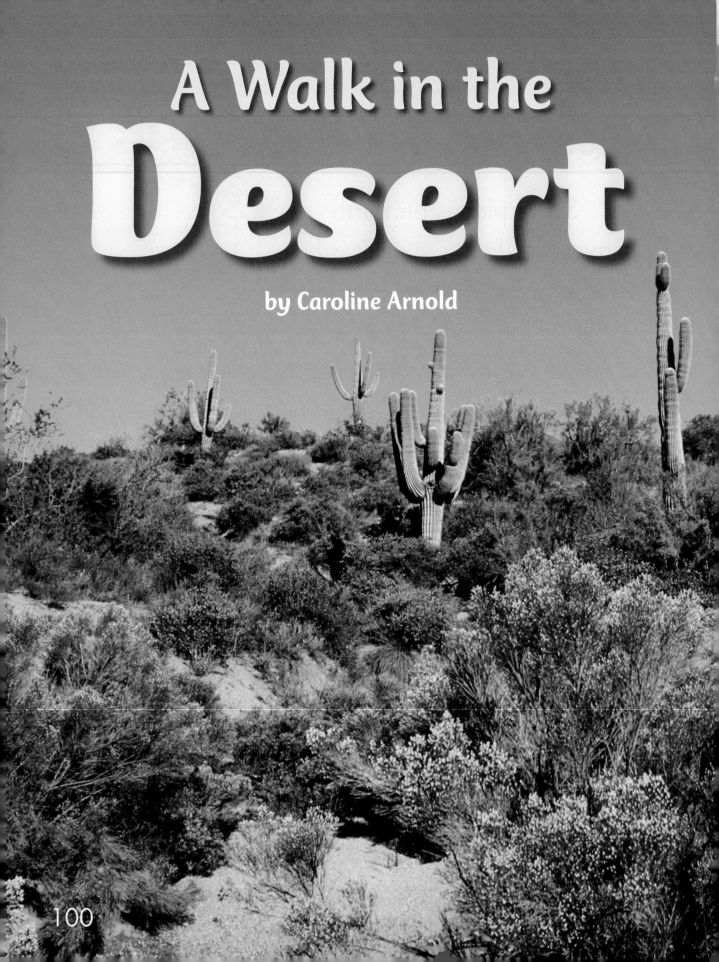

A Walk in the Desert

by Caroline Arnold

What can you find on a walk in the desert?

See the bright sun. Feel the dry air. It is hot—very hot! Where are we?

We're in the desert. Let's take a walk and see what we can find.

The ground is dry in the desert. It almost never rains. With so little water, it is hard for anything to live. But many plants and animals make their home in this harsh climate. You just have to look closely to see them.

Hedgehog Cactus

Teddy-Bear Cholla Cactus

Cactus is one kind of plant that grows in the desert. It doesn't have leaves. Instead, it has sharp spines. The spines protect the cactus from animals who might want to eat it. A cactus stores water in its stem. It uses the water when there is no rain.

Prickly Pear Cactus

Barrel Cactus

Saguaro Cactus

Look up at the tall saguaro. It is a giant among cactus plants. It took many years to grow so tall.

In late spring, white flowers bloom. Birds and insects drink the flowers' sweet nectar. After the flowers die, a red fruit grows.

Prickly Pear Fruit

Saguaro Cactus with White Flowers

Hawk

The saguaro cactus is home to many desert creatures. *Tap, tap, tap,* pecks a woodpecker. It is carving a hole for its nest. Old holes become nests for other birds.

A hawk is searching for food below. Its sharp eyes can spot even a tiny mouse.

Woodpecker

Owl

What is that large bird? It's a roadrunner. *Coo, coo, coo,* it calls. The roadrunner hardly ever flies, but it can run fast. Watch it chase a lizard to eat.

Roadrunner

Tree Lizard

Here are some other lizards. Lizards need the sun's heat to warm their scaly bodies. But when it gets too hot, they look for shade.

Zebra-Tailed Lizard

Leopard Lizard

Short-Horned Lizard

A rattlesnake lies next to a rock. Its earth colors make it hard to see. Rattlesnakes are dangerous. A bite from one will kill a small animal. If you hear a rattlesnake shake its tail, it is trying to scare you away.

Look! Did you see that rock move? It isn't a rock at all. It's a desert tortoise. The hard shell protects the tortoise from enemies and from the hot sun. The tortoise uses its sharp beak to break off tough desert grasses. It sometimes eats cactus fruits, too.

Rattlesnake

Cactus Fruits

Desert Tortoise

111

The jack rabbit is also a plant eater. Watch it sniff the early evening air. It is alert to the sounds and smells of the desert. When danger is near, the jack rabbit's long legs help it to escape quickly.

Jack Rabbits

As night begins to fall, the desert air cools. Animals who were hidden or sleeping come out to hunt and feed. A hungry coyote howls to the moon.

Do you see the small kit fox? Big ears help the fox to hear well so it can track animals to eat.

The cool night is full of activity.

Kangaroo Rat

Small Kit Fox